Kate's Garden

'What did you do at school today?' asked Mum.

'We were growing things,' said Kate. 'We put some water in a jam-jar. Then we put in some blotting paper and a bean. We're going to watch how it grows and make drawings of it.'

'Beans don't grow. They come in a tin from the shop,' said Jo, Kate's sister.

'You're thinking of baked beans,' said Kate, 'but these are a different sort of beans. They are called broad beans.'

Mum laughed. 'Baked beans grow too,' she said. 'They have to be picked and cooked and put into their tins. Most food is grown from seeds.'

'I like growing things,' said Kate. 'Can I have a bit of garden so I can grow some flowers?'

'I should think so,' said Mum.

'I'd like a garden too,' said Jo, 'but I'm going to grow things to eat.'

So Mum went down the garden with Kate and Jo and marked out two squares with sticks and string.

The squares were at the bottom of the vegetable garden. Nothing had grown there for a long time so the ground was very hard. It was covered in weeds.

'First you must dig out all the weeds. Then you must dig up the soil and take out any big stones.' The girls worked until it was bed-time. When it was time to go in there were still a lot of weeds left.

'Never mind,' said Mum. 'Gardening is very hard work. You can do some more tomorrow.'

Kate and Jo worked all through the weekend. ‘It’s beginning to look like a proper garden at last,’ said Kate.

‘It doesn’t look like a garden to me,’ said Jo. ‘Shouldn’t it have things growing in it?’

‘It will be better when we’ve put in the plants,’ said Kate.

Mum had a surprise for the girls when she collected them from school on Monday afternoon. ‘We’re going to the Garden Centre,’ she said.

The Garden Centre was behind the Supermarket. Some of the plants were in big greenhouses. Others were in the open air. There were trees and bushes, bulbs, packets of seeds, seedlings, pot plants, and lots of tomato plants.

'You can look round and choose what you want to grow,' said Mum. 'There are pictures of what the flowers will look like on the seed packets.'

Kate chose some poppy seeds and Jo chose lettuce and sunflower seeds.

'I think it's best if you plant the seeds in seed-boxes in the greenhouse,' said Mum. 'You can plant them outside when you see they have started to grow.' She showed the girls what to do. Kate and Jo planted their seeds and watered them. Then it was time for bed.

Next morning Kate said, 'Let's go and look at our seeds.' They went and inspected the boxes but they looked just the same. 'Perhaps we did something wrong,' she said.

'I can't even see mine,' said Jo. She began to poke the soil but there was no sign of any plants.

'Perhaps we planted them upside down,' said Jo. 'Perhaps they're growing downwards. Let's dig them up and have a look.' The two girls searched in the seed-boxes but they couldn't find any plants.

'I expect it takes a few days for them to grow,' suggested Kate. 'We'll give them some more water and try again tomorrow.' Every day they looked for the plants but nothing seemed to be happening.

One day Mum asked, 'How are your seeds coming along, Kate?'

'I don't think they're any good,' said Kate. 'We have been digging them up every day and we've given them buckets of water but they don't seem to work.'

'Good heavens!' laughed Mum. 'I'm not surprised. Seeds can't grow if you keep digging them up to look at them. I think we had better try again.'

So Mum took them back to the Garden Centre. This time they chose plants instead of seeds.

Jo chose some lettuce plants and Kate chose some pansies and some marigolds. ‘I think this will be easier,’ said Mum. ‘You can put these plants into your gardens straightaway. The lettuces should be ready in a few weeks and the flowers should be out in a month or two.’

‘But that’s ages!’ gasped Jo. ‘I’ll never be able to wait that long!’

‘If you want to be gardeners,’ laughed Mum, ‘you’ll just have to learn to be patient.’

Kate and Jo tried again. They pulled out the weeds that had started to grow in their gardens and they planted their flowers and lettuces in neat rows. Then they watered them very carefully. All seemed to be going well for a time. Kate's flowers grew bigger and little buds began to appear.

Jo's lettuces grew well at first. Then they stopped growing. 'I don't know what's gone wrong with my lettuces,' she said. 'First they stopped growing and now they're growing smaller.'

Mum came to look at the girls' gardens. 'Oh dear,' she said. 'Kate's flowers are doing well but I'm afraid the slugs have been eating your lettuces, Jo.'

'All that hard work for nothing!' said Jo. 'Why did they pick on me?'

'Well, there are some things slugs like to eat and some things they don't. They like lettuces but they don't like pansies and marigolds.'

'It's not fair!' said Jo. 'Now I'll have to start all over again.'

The next afternoon Jo dug up the remains of the lettuces and threw them on the compost heap.

'What are you going to plant this time?' asked her sister.

'I'm not telling you. It's a secret,' said Jo. 'It's something that slugs won't want to eat. I've never heard of slugs eating what I'm going to grow.'

Jo spent the next evening digging up her garden again. She planted something under the soil, but she wouldn't tell Kate what it was.

In a few weeks Kate's flowers began to open. Jo watered her garden every day but there was no sign of anything growing.

'What did you plant?' asked Kate again.

'I'm not telling,' said Jo. 'They should have started growing by now but I'm not going to dig them up to see. I'm being patient.'

At the weekend Dad came to look at the two gardens. 'Kate's flowers are lovely,' he said. 'But what about yours, Jo? I can't see very much happening on your plot.'

Jo looked as if she was going to cry. 'I've just got to keep being patient,' she said.

'But what did you plant?' asked Dad.

'Sweets,' whispered Jo.

'Sweets,' said Dad. He smiled to himself. 'Yes, you'll just have to be patient,' he said.

The next morning Kate and Jo went to look at their gardens before they went to school. 'Look!' shouted Jo. 'They've grown at last!' There were twigs all over Jo's patch and some had sweets on them.

'That's funny,' said Kate, 'I didn't think sweets grew on twigs. And they've got wrappers on them.'

'It's even funnier,' said Jo. 'They've all come up toffees and I planted fruit gums.'

'Someone has played a trick on you,' said Kate.

'I don't care,' said Jo. 'I like toffees better than lettuces.'

All About Seeds

There are seeds of all shapes and sizes. A bean is a seed and so is an apple pip. Some seeds are so tiny that you can hardly see them. All seeds are alike in two ways. Every seed contains a tiny plant and every seed contains enough food to start the plant growing.

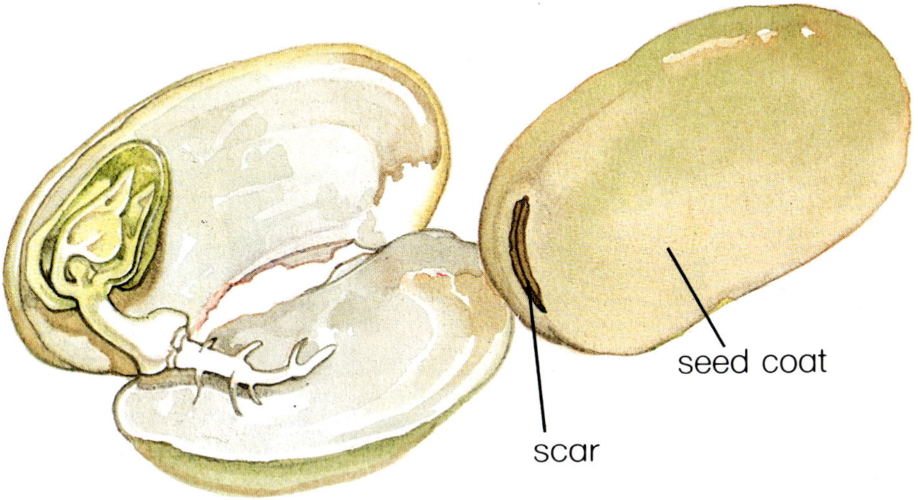

A seed has a hard coat to protect the tiny plant that will grow inside it. In the hard coat there is a tiny hole. Through the hole the seed gets the moisture that will help it to start growing. On all seeds you should be able to find a tiny scar. The scar shows where the seed was once joined to the fruit in which it grew.

Apart from moisture a seed needs two other things before it will germinate. Germinate means 'start to grow'. These two things are air and warmth. Why do you think so many seeds start to grow in spring?

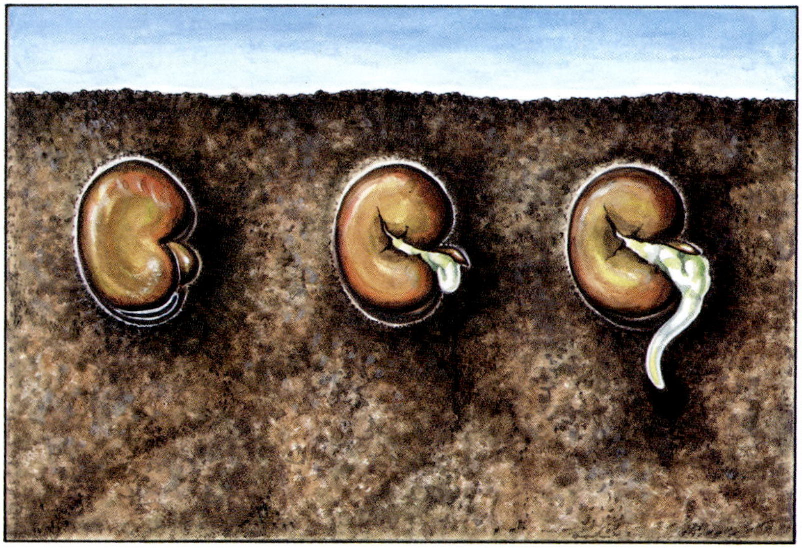

All seeds come from flowers. Some plants have only one flower at the top of a single stem. How many plants can you think of which have only one flower? Other plants, such as bluebells, have many flowers. How many examples can you think of? Trees and grasses also have flowers. These flowers are often green, so you may not have noticed them.

Sweets are not plants and they don't have flowers. You can't grow them in your garden. But many of the things sweets are made from are grown from seeds. Can you find out what these things are, and where they are grown?

The Wise Chicken

A hungry chicken was once scratching around the farmyard looking for something to eat. All she could find were a few grains of wheat. She was about to eat them when she had a good idea. ‘If I plant this wheat,’ she thought, ‘it will grow and I shall be able to make bread. It will be hard work and it will take a long time, but it will be worth it.’

The chicken decided to ask her friends to help her with the work.

'Would anybody like to help me plant this wheat?' asked the chicken.

'Sorry,' said the cat. 'I'm going to have dinner with a family of mice that has just moved into the old barn.'

'I'd like to help,' said the duck, 'but it's such a nice day. I think I'll go for a swim.'

'Too bad!' said the dog. 'I have to bring the sheep down from the meadow. Perhaps another time.'

'I'll have to do it myself,' thought the chicken.

After a long time the seeds had grown into a big patch of golden wheat. 'Look at my wonderful wheat!' laughed the chicken. 'We'll soon have plenty to eat. Who is going to help me cut it down?'

'Well, I'd like to,' said the cat, 'but I've got a sore paw.'

'I have to rest,' said the duck. 'I think I'm going to lay an egg.'

'It's too hot to work,' complained the dog.

'I'll have to do it myself,' thought the chicken.

The cat, the duck, and the dog sat in the sunshine and watched the little chicken cutting down the corn. It took her all afternoon and she looked very hot and tired when she had finished.

'I think we should disappear,' whispered the cat to the dog and the duck. 'I'll bet she's going to ask us to help grind the wheat into flour.'

'Who would like to help me grind . . . ' called the chicken. But before she had finished the sentence, the dog, the cat, and the duck had gone.

Next morning there was a delicious smell of baking bread in the farmyard. The cat, the dog, and the duck went to visit their friend, the chicken. She was just taking a crisp, golden loaf out of the oven. 'Hello,' said the chicken. 'I suppose you're all hungry.'

'Starving,' said the cat.

'Famished,' said the dog.

'I must admit that I'm a little peckish,' smiled the duck. 'Your bread smells delicious, and there's so much of it. Would you like us to help you eat it?'

'No thanks,' laughed the chicken, 'I think I can manage on my own.'

The Gift of Corn

Nobody knows how or when people discovered the secret of planting and growing crops. A Canadian Indian tribe tell this story to explain the mystery.

A long time ago, the first people to live in Canada did not know how to grow corn. They hunted animals in the forests and on the plains. They caught fish in the rivers and lakes and they collected nuts and berries in the woods.

By the side of a lake lived a Chief and his tribe. For many years they hunted and fished and had plenty to eat. Many children were born and the tribe grew bigger and bigger and everybody was happy.

Then, one year, came a terrible winter. It started early and when the time for spring had come, ice still covered the lake and the rivers and the animals died in the forest because they had nothing to eat.

The tribe grew hungrier and hungrier until, one day, the Chief called them all together and this is what he said.

'The winter has been long and cold, and our stores of food are almost used up. There are few animals left in the forests and each day our hunters return empty-handed. We catch no fish because the ice on the rivers and on the lake is too thick to break. You must leave this place and travel to the warm lands of the south in search of food. I shall stay here to protect this land from our enemies. When the winter has gone, I shall come and find you, and bring you home again.'

When the tribe had gone, their Chief sat in front of his fire and wondered what to do. After a while his fire burned low and went out and he felt cold, miserable, and hungry.

Suddenly, a little man stepped out of the forest. He had a golden skin and wore a red feather in his head-band. He sat down in front of the Chief and begged him to say why his village was deserted and why he sat alone by the ashes of his fire.

The Chief told his story. When he had finished the little man said, 'My name is Red Feather. You must come with me to a clearing in the forest and wrestle with me. If I win, your tribe will never return to live by the side of the lake but if you can throw me down on the Earth, your tribe shall live here happily, and never feel hunger again.'

The Chief followed Red Feather into the forest and the two men began to wrestle. Red Feather was small but he was very strong, and the Chief was weak with hunger. The contest went on for the rest of the afternoon, and all night long, but when the next day began to break, the Chief made one last great effort and threw Red Feather to the Earth.

'I've won! I've won!' he cried. The Chief stretched out his hand to help Red Feather to his feet, but the little man had disappeared. Lying on the ground where he had fallen was a small object, shaped like a pine cone. It was covered in what looked like hard yellow stones.

Then the Chief thought the Wind spoke to him. 'Pull the yellow seeds from the husk,' said the voice in the wind, 'and scatter them on the Earth.'

The Chief did as the voice told him. As he was scattering the yellow seeds the voice spoke again. 'Come back here in a month,' it said.

As the days passed the sun began to warm the land and the snow melted. When a month had gone by the Chief returned to the clearing in the forest. He saw that where he had scattered the seeds the ground was covered in bright green shoots. Again he heard a voice. This time it seemed to come from the shoots themselves as they whispered in the warm breeze. 'Come back in five months,' they seemed to say. 'We are not ready for you yet.'

On a hot day at the end of the summer the Chief returned again to the clearing in the forest. Where the green shoots had been, was a field of golden corn. On each ear of corn grew a bright red plume.

The voice in the cornfield told the Chief how to harvest the corn cobs and how to grind the corn into flour. He learned how to save some of the seeds for the next year's planting, and how to store the rest for food during the winter months.

When he had harvested all the corn the Chief went to lead back his tribe to their home by the lake. There they lived in happiness and were never hungry again.